Trombone

THE BAND METHOD THAT TEACHES MUSIC READING

RHYTHM MASTER

Supplemental Material

T0078554

By

J.R. McEntyre
Coordinator of Music, Retired
Odessa Public Schools
Odessa, Texas

And

Harry H. Haines
Music Department Chairman
West Texas State University
Canyon, Texas

Trombone Position Chart

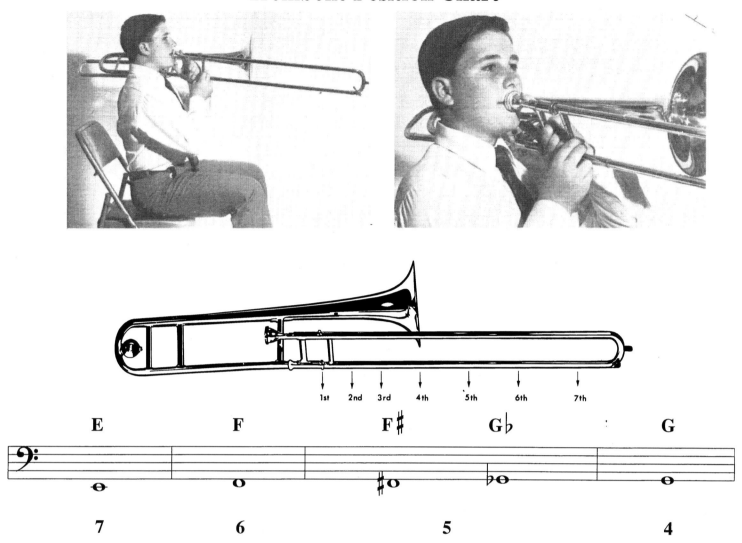

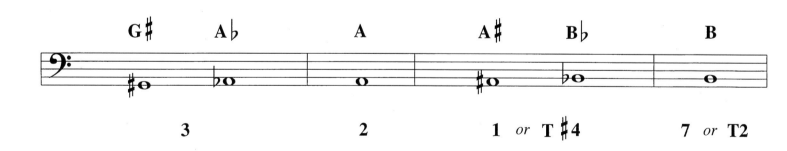

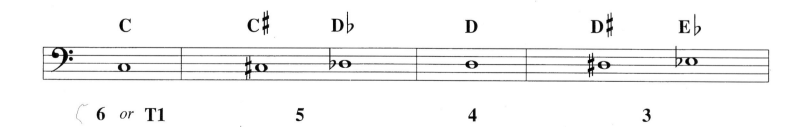

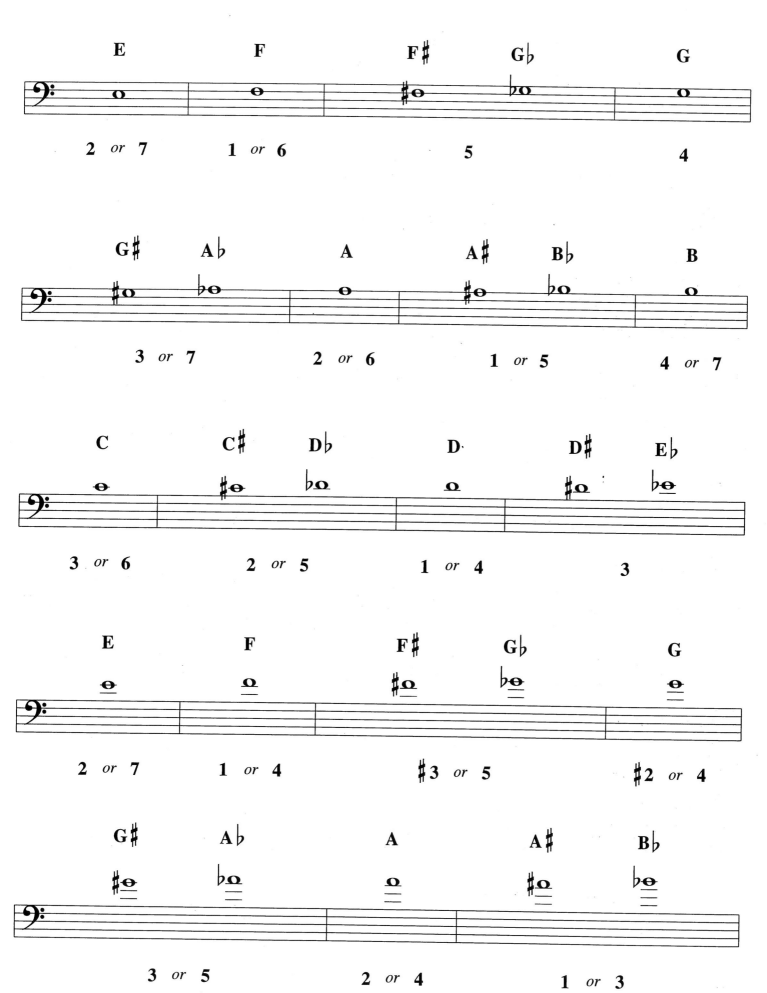

LESSON 1
Concert F

These "flag" symbols indicate something new. New notes are flagged as "NEW."

A numbered flag refers to the **Index of Musical Terms** on the back cover.

⌐⌐ = *whole step*

∨ = *half step*

1 Tetrachord on F

tetrachord ascending

tetrachord descending

2 Chalameau-Clarion Etude

3 Chromatic Exercise *Do this first in four beats per measure, then in two beats.*

or

Watch out!

4 Chalameau to My Lou

5 Simple Gifts

6 Jason and Jennifer Duet

7 Duet Part

LESSON 2
Concert B Flat

27 *sharp*

1 **Tetrachord on B Flat**

2 **B Flat Major Scale** *The two tetrachords are a whole step apart.* **3** *arpeggio*

B flat
tetrachord — — — — *F tetrachord*

3 **Clarinets Right Hand Down** *Play this line slowly, then play it in 2/2 time.*

or

4 **Chromatic Exercise**

NEW

5 **High School Cadets**

1. 2.

6 **Rocky Mountain Duet**

7 **Duet Part**

LESSON 3
Concert E Flat

1 **Tetrachord on E Flat**

2 **Chalameau-Clarion Etude**

3 **Chromatic Exercise**

4 **Amazing Grace**

5 **Grandfather's Clock**

6 **Menuet Duet**

7 **Duet Part**

8 **Little Fugue** 4

Part One

Part Two

Part Three

LESSON 4
Concert A Flat

D♭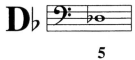

5

1a The New Note
NEW

1b Enharmonic Note

1c Enharmonic Etude

2 Tetrachord on A Flat

3 Major Scale on A Flat

A flat tetrachord ------- *E flat tetrachord*

4 Chromatic Exercise

5 Tune in A Flat Concert

1.   2.

6 Long Long Ago

6 *double repeat measure*

LESSON 5
Changing Keys Lesson

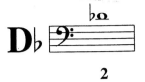

1 **Yankee in F Concert**

2 **Yankee in B Flat Concert**

3 **Yankee in E Flat Concert**

4 **Yankee in A Flat Concert**

5 **March in F Major**

6 **Buffalo Gals**

7 **Loch Lomond**

8 **Amaryllis**

Rhythm Set #1
Eighth, Quarter, and Dotted Quarter Rhythms

LESSON 6
Dotted Quarter Note Review

D

1 Rhythmic Precision

NEW

2 Duet Part

3 Clarinet Help

4 Auld Lang Syne

7

%

1. 2. *Fine*

8 *D.S. al Fine*

5 Crazy Rhythm Duet *Can you name the song?*

6 Duet Part

7 Dotted Quarter Round

1

2

3

LESSON 7
More Dotted Quarter Notes

F#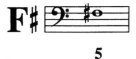
5

1 Dotted Quarter Duo

2 Duet Part

3 Chromatic Exercise

NEW

Watch out!

4 Men of Harlech

5 Deck the Halls

6 Dotted Quarter Song

7 Accompaniment

LESSON 8
Syncopation Review

1 Syncopation

2 Duet Part

3 Syncopation Scale

HERE'S HELP: If you're having trouble, count, and play, Rhythm Set #2. Then come back to these lines.

4 Syncopated Chromatic   *Careful!*

5 Tom Dooley

6 That's Where My Money Goes

7 Old Gray Mare

8 New Gray Mare (Crazy Rhythm)

LESSON 9
Harder Syncopation

1 Multiple Syncopation *Play separately, then together.*

2 Duet Part

SUGGESTION: If you're having trouble, count, and play, Rhythm Set #2. Then come back to these lines.

3 Concert D Flat

4 Chromatic Drill
or

5 Red River Valley

6 Cindy

7 You're a Grand Old Flag

Can you count, and play, this entire page without stopping?

SUGGESTION: Look ahead. While you finish one rhythm, look at the next.

1

2

3

4

5

6

7

8

9

10

11

12

13

14

15

16

17

18

19

20

21

22

23

24

25

26

27

28

29

30

31

32

33

34

35

36

B-502

LESSON 10
The Enharmonic Lesson

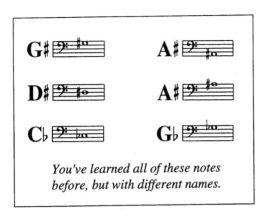

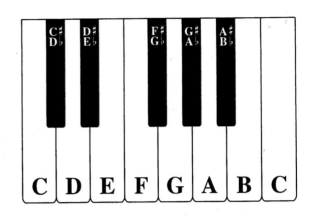

You've learned all of these notes before, but with different names.

This keyboard will help you to learn which notes are enharmonic.

5

1a The Note

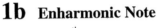

1b Enharmonic Note

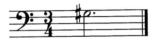

1c Enharmonic Etude

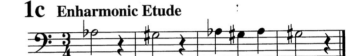

2 Enharmonic Echo

3 Echo Part

4 Ascending and Descending Chromatic Scales

5 Bill Bailey Won't You Please Come Home?

NEW

LESSON 11
Sixteenth Notes

1 Rhythmic Scale

2 Part Two

3 Echo Song

4 Part Two

5 Music in the Air

6 Polly Wolly Doodle

7 Frere Jacques (Round)

B-502

Rhythm Set #3
Sixteenth Note Rhythms

LESSON 12
More Sixteenth Notes

1 **Rhythmic Challenge**

2 **Duet Part**

3 **Chromatic Scale Review**

Really good players can play the chromatic scale from memory. Can you?

4 **Mixed Up Echo**

5 **Duet Part**

6 **Skip to My Lou**

7 **Up on the Housetop**

8 **Someone's in the Kitchen with Dinah**

LESSON 13
Dotted Eighth Lesson

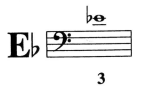

1 Thinking Sixteenths

2 The Sixteenth Rest **10**

3 More Sixteenth Rests

4 Dotted Eighth and Sixteenth **11**

5 O Christmas Tree

6 Here Comes the Bride

NEW

7 College Song

8 Clementine

Rhythm Set #4
Dotted Eighth and Sixteenth Rhythms

B-502

LESSON 14
Dotted Eighths and Dotted Quarters

1 Dotted Scale

2 Dotted Duo

3 Duet Part

4 Railroad Song

5 March of the Kings

6 Rueben (Crazy Rhythm Duet)

7 Rachel

LESSON 15
Adding Dynamics

LESSON 16
Rhythmic Review

1 Rhythmic Review

2 On the Beat

3 Off the Beat

4 Merrily All Mixed Up (Crazy Rhythm)

5 This Old Man

mf

6 This New Man

mf

7 American Patrol

pp

8 Accompaniment

21 *crescendo poco a poco*

pp

f

f

crescendo

ff

ff

LESSON 17
The Concert D Flat Lesson

1 Concert D Flat Scale

A flat tetrachord

D flat tetrachord

REMINDER: *A major scale is two tetrachords one whole step apart.*

2 Thirds

3 This Old Man

mf

4 Skip to My Lou

mf

5 Auld Lang Syne

f

A

6 Duet Part

f

B

C

LESSON 18
The Concert C Lesson

LESSON 19
Changing Keys

1 **Billy Boy in D Flat Concert**

2 **Billy Boy in C Concert**

3 **Kum Bah Yah in F Concert**

4 **Dixie in B Flat Concert**

5 **Alouette in E Flat Concert**

6 **Country Gardens in A Flat Concert**

LESSON 20
6/8 Time Lesson

Rhythm Set #5
Compound Time Rhythms

B-502

LESSON 21
3/8 Time Lesson

You've learned this note before, but with a different name.

1 3/8 Exercise

2 3/8 Etude

3 Chromatic Scale in 3/8

4 Back Down Again

5 Halloween Song

6 The Man on the Flying Trapeze

7 Three Blind Mice (Round)

B-502

29

LESSON 22
6/8 Time Is Easy

LESSON 23
The Last Lesson!

1 Scale in 9/8

2 Scale in 12/8

3 Morning Song

4 Sorcerer's Apprentice   *What is the last note of the first measure?*

5 The Last Song

6 Accompaniment

Scale Page

All major scales consist of two tetrachords with one whole step in between. A tetrachord consists of four notes with a whole step between notes one and two, a whole step between notes two and three, and a half step between notes three and four.

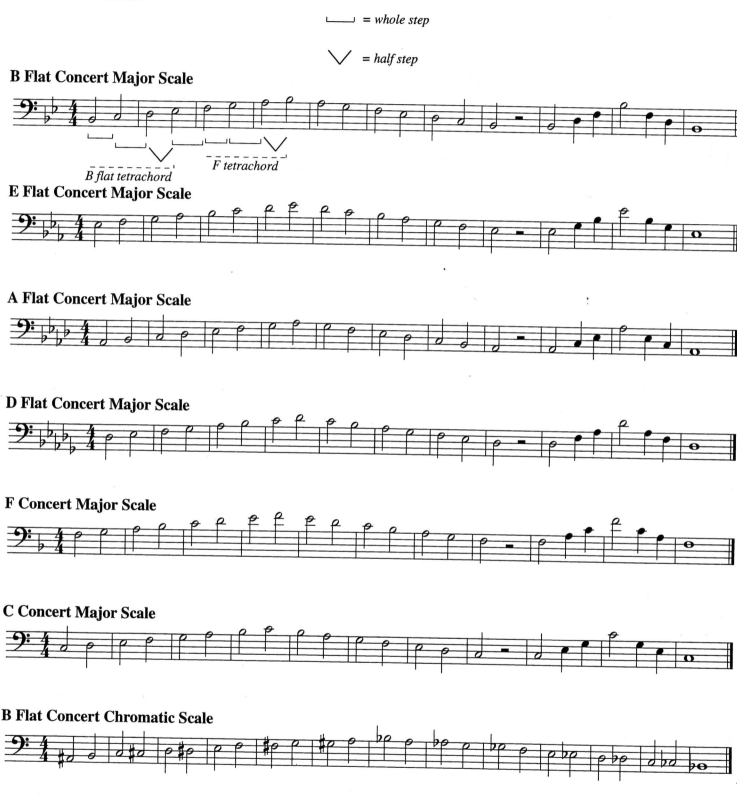

After learning these scales <u>accurately</u>, practice in a variety of rhythm patterns. Work for even execution and faster and faster tempi.

Practice Record Chart

Week	Day 1	Day 2	Day 3	Day 4	Day 5	Day 6	Day 7	Total Time	Parent's Initials	Weekly Grade	Week	Day 1	Day 2	Day 3	Day 4	Day 5	Day 6	Day 7	Total Time	Parent's Initials	Weekly Grade
1											19										
2											20										
3											21										
4											22										
5											23										
6											24										
7											25										
8											26										
9											27										
10											28										
11											29										
12											30										
13											31										
14											32										
15											33										
16											34										
17											35										
18											36										

Index of Musical Terms

1 **Tetrachord** - the first four notes of a major scale or any four notes that are linked with the following intervals: whole step, whole step, half step

2 **Chromatic** - an interval between two notes that is a half step

3 **Arpeggio** - the notes of a chord played one at a time

4 **Fugue** - a composition in which a melody is imitated by several different instruments; if the melody is imitated exactly, the composition is a cannon

5 **Enharmonic** - different names for the same note; G sharp and A flat are the same note, therefore they are enharmonic

6 **Double Repeat Measure** - means to repeat the preceding two measures

7 **Del Signo Sign** - indicates where to play after reaching D.S. al Fine (see #8)

8 **D.S. al Fine** - means to go back to the Del Signo Sign and play until "Fine" is reached

9 **Sixteenth Note** - gets one fourth of a beat in any time signature with a 4 as the bottom numeral

10 **Sixteenth Rest** - gets one fourth of a beat in any time signature with a 4 as the bottom numeral

11 **Dotted Eighth Note** - gets three fourths of a beat in any time signature with a 4 as the bottom numeral; equivalent to three sixteenth notes

12 **Dotted Eighth Rest** - gets three fourths of a beat in any time signature with a 4 as the bottom numeral; equivalent to three sixteenth rests

f **13** **Forte** - means to play loudly

p **14** **Piano** - means to play softly

pp **15** **Pianissimo** - means to play very softly

mp **16** **Mezzo Piano** - means to play moderately soft

mf **17** **Mezzo Forte** - means to play moderately loud

ff **18** **Fortissimo** - means to play very loudly

19 **Crescendo Sign** - means to play gradually louder

20 **Decrescendo (or Diminuendo) Sign** - means to play gradually softer

21 **Crescendo Poco a Poco** - the word crescendo means the same as the crescendo sign; poco a poco means little by little; the words are often used instead of the sign when a long crescendo is needed

22 **6/8 Time Signature** - two beats in each measure; each dotted quarter note gets one beat

23 **3/8 Time Signature** - one beat in each measure; each dotted quarter note gets one beat

24 **9/8 Time Signature** - three beats in each measure; each dotted quarter note gets one beat

25 **12/8 Time Signature** - four beats in each measure; each dotted quarter note gets one beat

♭ **26** **Flat** - lowers a note one half step

♯ **27** **Sharp** - raises a note one half step

34

Warm-ups

Play a good, strong tone.

Look up any unfamiliar notes in the ***Fingering Chart*** *on pages 2 and 3.*

Warm-up #1

Warm-up #2

Warm-up #3 *Practice slowly! Work for smooth, even slurs.*

Warm-up #4

Warm-up #5 *Practice slowly! Keep the airstream flowing smoothly! It's the quality of the slur that is most importan*

Warm-up #6 *Practice slowly at first. If necessary, play each note as an eighth, then as a sixteenth.*

Selected Trombone/ Euphonium Publications

METHODS

MARSTELLER, ROBERT

B268   **Basic Routines**   HL3770381

A volume of calisthenic exercises compiled to assist in the muscle development used in playing the trombone.Exercises are broken into four sections: (1)Attack and tome placement; (2) Slow Slurs; (3) Flexibility; (4) Scales and Arpeggios

COLLECTIONS

BACH, J.S.

Marsteller, Robert

B403   **Six Suites, Bk. 1 (Suites 1, 2, 3)**   HL3770615

The set of six Suites for Violoncello Solo is a monumental masterpiece of the Baroque Period. This edition for trombone, baritone or bassoon presents the Suites in their original keys. Optional notes for the use of the Bass Trombone, or any instrument with an "F" attachment, are noted.

BORDOGNI, GIULIO

Hoffman, Earl

B385   **17 Vocalises**   HL3770586

The vocalises by Marco Bordogni provide excellent practice material for trombone students. In order to make these melodious exercises even more interesting for both the student and the teacher, the arranger has composed second parts in contrapuntal form resulting in duets which are pleasing as well as practical. The added second part is generally somewhat more difficult than the original and may be considered to be the teacher's part. However, as the student progresses, they should master both parts. Theses pieces may also be performed by other like bass clef instruments.

SOLO WITH PIANO

BARAT, J.E.

SS361   **Andante et Allegro**   HL3773993

BARAT, J.E.

Smith, Glenn E.

SS974   **Introduction and Dance**   HL3774665

BELLSTEDT, HERMAN

Simon, Frank

SS371   **Napoli**   HL3774006

Napoli is perhaps the most famous solo by Sousa arranger and cornet virtuoso Hermann Bellstedt. Conceived as a theme and variations on a wildly popular 19th Century song, this edition by Bellstedt's student and Sousa band successor Frank Simon remains the one most performed today. This edition for trombone and euphonium by Tommy Fry comes with both bass and treble clef barts.

DAVIS, WILLIAM MAC

ST444   **Variations on a Theme Of Robert Schumann**   HL3775131

Concert band accompaniment also published by Southern Music. (S537CB)

EWAZEN, ERIC

SU450   **Ballade for Bass or Tenor Trombone (reduction)**   HL3776369

Ballade for Bass or Tenor Trombone is based on an earlier work for clarinet and string orchestra. This arrangement was written for Charles Vernon of the Chicago Symphony in 1996, who later recorded the work on Albany Records (Troy 479). Comes with separate bass and tenor trombone parts. Duration ca. 12'.

SU339   **Concerto No. 1 for Trombone (Sonata for Trombone)**   HL3776236

Completed in the Spring of 1993, Ewazen's Sonata for Trombone was commissioned by Michael Powell who premiered the work at the Aspen Music Festival and recorded it on Cala Records. Later orchestra and band arrangements followed, both of which feature an added cadenza and are available separately from the publisher. Duration ca. 18', Grade 5.

HANDEL, GEORGE FRIDERIC

Powell, Richard

SS827   **Sonata No. 3**   HL3774492

The only edition of this work that includes a Bb treble solo part for trumpet or euphonium in addition to the bass clef part. Originally for flute, this five movement sonata is an ideal recital piece; lengthy enough to be considered a major work, varied enough to prove the performer's ability in technique, sound, control, range and musicianship; yet not so difficult to be out of the range of the average high school trombonist.

MARCELLO, BENEDETTO

Merriman, Lyle

SS806   **Adagio and Allegro**   HL3774474

SS807   **Largo and Allegro**   HL3774475

MOZART, WOLFGANG AMADEUS

Marsteller, Robert

ST94   **Concerto in B-flat, K191 (B flat Major)**   HL3775812

Transcribed by one of the great American trombonists of the 20th Century, Robert Marsteller, longtime player with the LA Philharmonic after World War II. This concerto, originally for bassoon, features delightful but challenging passages for the advanced trombonist.

MOZART, WOLFGANG AMADEUS

Powell, Richard

SS842   **Arietta and Allegro, K109B/8 K3**   HL3774509

NUX, PAUL VERONGE DE LA

SS145   **Concert Piece**   HL3773749

An andante-allegro work in a single movement edition inscribed for the National School Music Competition-Festivals.

SENAILLE, JEAN BAPTISTE

Falcone, Leonard

SS563   **Allegro Spiritoso**   HL3774203

The "Allegro Spiritoso" is the 3rd movement of a Sonata in D Minor. This well known piece is arranged for baritone, euphonium, or trombone. Both bass clef and treble clef parts are provided. Versions for following instruments are available from the publisher: alto clarinet, bass clarinet, contra alto clarinet, contrabass clarinet, alto saxophone, tenor saxophone, baritone saxophone, bassoon, euphonium/trombone, and tuba.

SPEARS, JARED

ST311   **Ritual and Celebration**   HL3774957

The character of the "Ritual" movement is dramatic and slow, which trasitions without pause to the quick and lively "Celebration". Commissioned by and dedicated to Ken Kistner.

TRIO

MENDELSSOHN, FELIX

Collins, Wilbur

ST350   **Lift Thine Eyes**   HL3775004

Exclusively distributed by    Questions/ comments? info@laurenkeisermusic.com